VASU - MY BESTIE

FROM BEST FRIENDS TO STRANGERS

HANSINI PUNJ

For my Bestie, "Vasu"

Hansini Punj, who wrote the book " Vasu- My Bestie " is entirtely dedicated to my best friend.

NOTE TO MY BEST FRIEND :

वसुदेवसुतं देवं कंसचाणूरमर्दनं। देवकी परमानन्दम कृष्णं वंदे जगदगुरुम
|| ॐ ॐ ॐ

चन्दनं शीतलं लोके,चन्दनादपि चन्द्रमाः !

चन्द्रचन्दनयोर्मध्ये शीतला साधुसंगतिः !!

Sandalwood is considered to be the coolest in this world, but the moon is cooler than sandalwood, but a good friend is cooler than both the moon and sandalwood.

Vasu, I'm truly blessed to be able to meet you. You're my bestie and will always remain. I'm falling short of words to say anything. I'm filled with lots of gratitude.

I just want to say that

"I carry thoughts of you like my own personal constellation. How far away you are, my dearest best friend, but no farther than those fixed stars in my soul."

Contents

Preface

Fellow readers, you're gonna read events that are based on true incidents, which is the most precious part of my life, whom we call " best friends" . Now, who are best friends ? Best friends are someone who is very close to you and something that you can't afford to lose, someone with whom you share the darkest stories of your life and things that you don't even tell your parents. Before delving into my life's precious journey, get a sneak- peek into my life and today's scenario that still curtails women's freedom.

Prologue

It is said not all stories have a happy ending because it's not a film. The pinching sensation, when he left me without even saying Goodbye. Some of my fellow readers might relate when bestfriens leave you all alone. It becomes all the more hurting when he didn't even bother to tell me the reason as to why he left me. I'm completely shattered inot pieces. The more sorrowful part is seeing him happily posting stories and getting busy in life. It seems as he has forgotten everything and as if I dont even exist for him. I just want to see him progressing in life. Even if he has forgotten him I smile to see him happy and in good health. I wish him abundance of success ahead.

CHAPTER ONE

MY INTRODUCTION

I'm a simple Delhi girl full of ambitions and a very emotional being. To be more specific, a History student and an Archaeology enthusiast. Since seventh standard, I have developed immense Interest and passion in History and Archaeology. I have done research and written articles on various historical issues. One such article is Herodotus - The Father of History. I identify myself as an introverted person who doesn't have many friends. But an unexpected meeting with a person (devotee) changed everything. He became my bestie, my devotee friend, my brother, my teacher, my guide, my moral supporter, my human diary, my walkie - talkie, my cheerleader, my comfort space and the one whom I admire the most.

CHAPTER TWO

MOTIVE BEHIND THE TITLE

You must be thinking why the title of this story is " Best friends to strangers". Well, there are situations which happened with many of you where your best friend leaves you and that situation is really heart-breaking. One such pinching thing, unfortunately happened to me as well. Some might relate to this situation.

Before proceeding further in this story, let us know more about me. Here, I'm detailing my nature and personality which will help you connect with the story. I'm a very sensitive person. Since childhood I've been caged to a limited area of connections. I grew up in an environment with so many restrictions. I've been exposed to an unhealthy atmosphere, a mysognist society filled with violence and patriarchy. I was told from the start to not talk to boys as it's not appropriate for a good girl in a male dominating society. I'm telling you frankly, I could not be a "good girl". Studying in an all girls convent school where there was so much strictness owing to a disciplined environment. After passing out from high school, I went to a coed college. My family members were worried about me as it was against their custom to send me among boys.

They all told me to take a girl's college but I wanted a nice faculty where I can follow my passion. Now let me tell you one more thing, I belong to a family where the belief system revolves around the marriage of a girl child is very essential. I find it so creepy, marrying off a girl without her choice. It seems she has no life of her own. Her decisions do not matter. She doesn't even have a choice, an independent life.

CHAPTER THREE

ARISTOCRATS AND RESTRICTIONS

I'm a girl who does not accept these restrictions and so-called norms in this misogynist society. My parents do not want me to make male friends and if they see me talking to boys late at night, I'll be in pieces. I call this "aristocracy". I don't believe these norms and don't obey them. Yes, I'm wrong according to my parents and misogynist society. And it's absolutely normal to be wrong. We are living in the 21st century and still people are not open minded. I understand parents are worried about children's security. But that doesn't mean to cage your child. It is ironic how parents lay emphasis on being independent when they themselves don't leave their child independently. This mentality is just like

"birds without wings". In the end, they want children to earn a decent living and get married. But what about the passion, the dreams they were trying to fulfill ?

Passion and dreams are shattered and they have to obey their parents no matter what but because they are "parents".

CHAPTER FOUR

DREAMS- OUT OF REACH

Parents become so overprotective that in a way they kill a child's independence. The child then becomes a timid person with low self-esteem. And at this time, the child dies internally which no one tries to understand. From the beginning, we are told to run in a "rat race", killing your dreams to maintain the standard of a "good girl" in a society. A "good girl" should not be outside till night, should not have boyfriends and alway put her family over everything. I have friends in college who say that if they see them talking to boys, they'll kill them. One of the most popular line you all must have heard is "Ladki haath se nikal gayi". What becomes all the more worse when the concept of "right age to marry" comes. The dream of higher education becomes a mere thought. In India, there are very few women who could pursue a PHD. Some ambitious women in their late 30's or 40's pursue PHD only if their husband's family does not have any issues. In a world of injustice, pain and suffering be the light of your own world. Even a light takes time to glow. But when it glows it becomes a mirror. A mirror of real self, to outshine the real soul to make them rise in their own eyes.

CHAPTER FIVE

Realisation

Be a fighter not a prey of injustice. Be a sufferer instead of a victim. Make yourself a stone hearted in this world full of violence. Make yourself a deaf ear

To cope with mocking words of people

Make yourself a rock and not a rose for the people to tear you apart. Make yourself a hard coconut to not to come in people's words. Train yourself to cope with harsh reality and not be a delicate doll. For the people to make you use and throw.Be the smile of your own self to bring countless smiles who're suffering to make their lives sustainable. Tis the experience of an empty hollow soul seeking for knowledge

To make her rise in her own eyes.

Here my question arrives to you all : When will this mentality change? When can we see a change among parents?

CHAPTER SIX

An Empty Hollow Soul

This was the background with which you can relate to my story. My story begins when I was a student at school. I didn't have many friends. Many of them speak to me for help in assignments, study and homework but when their need was satisfied, they went. As I've said earlier, I am a very emotional being, I didn't get even a single friend who could talk to me, who cares about me or with whom I can relate and share my feelings. Mostly people ditched me and I couldn't do anything. I started developing anxiety and fear of being alone. Being in an unhealthy atmosphere full of fights at home, domestic violence, patriarchy and being alone at school left me devastated. As a result my personality became a timid girl with low self-esteem. When there is low self-esteem you cannot imagine the unpleasant condition I was facing. I consider myself as an empty hollow soul.

Seeking knowledge in the right direction. To see the rainbow of the bright future,

The light of purity glowing glittery in the night. I want to show the path to the unfortunate ones to make them a rising star In their own eyes. Noble men and artist come and go showing their ecstasy but what remains a hidden fact is their pain which is inside, crushing the inner feelings and pouring joy to outsiders.

CHAPTER SEVEN

MY PRECIOUS BESTIE

Now, in the year 2020, I was in twelfth standard. I made an instagram account for collecting Archaeological data for my History project. From then, I joined Krishna Bhakti groups as I'm a devotee of Krishna. I made many friends and during that time, I met my best friend, his name is

"Ayush Dubey" and his family name is "Vasudev". In the beginning, he sent many posts and reels . I just responded to them. Then we introduced ourselves and got to know that we are in the same class - twelfth standard. Our first call was indeed a special one as he insisted on talking on call about Vedic scriptures and I ignored him at first as I was scared then I talked on call with him. We both were nervous but laughed at jokes and all. Towards his side, crackers were bursting and he told me that it was our first call and in the background there were crackers bursting. After that We did general talk and found out our likes-dislikes.We talked about several matters on call. Gradually, I felt more connected to him and we started talking for longer durations. Sometimes late at night as well. We did video calls as well and we spent quality time together. I have never seen such a boy who is so decent, not like other boys who use abusive words. He respected females so much that he touched their feets and worshiped them like a "Devi". We played a questionnaire game to get to know each other better. He told me stories about the historical mahal "The Vir Singh Palace" . I was mesmerized hearing about this historic fort. I'm also interested in haunted stuff, so when I told him about a game called Ouija board, he installed Ouija board game from the Play Store and played it. It was fun. We kept nick-names for each other, I called him "Vasu". I found my comfort with him. It was the first time I found a friend who is not like others who talk to me just for help in studies. I considered myself lucky, blessed and felt as if Lord Krishna only made a situation to meet him. I made him my best friend. I shared my darkest secrets, my problems, my feelings to him and he is like a medicine to me. I'm the happiest I'm around him. Talking to him makes me feel relaxed and I forget all my worries and tensions. He is so gentle, soft and not like other boys who keeps flirting with many girls. He considers me as his sister and I was also blessed with a precious brother by soul and it was him, my "bestie". We talked everyday, I told him everything and when I was sad he made me comfortable and relaxed. Sometimes he cracked jokes while talking to make me happy. I was so overwhelmed to have him by my side. I adore him for his inner purity and a kind, caring and understanding individual that reflected his outward appearance. In today's world, it is very hard to find such a person. He is very rare, unique and pure.

CHAPTER EIGHT

DESOLATION

Happy moments turned into misery when my mother didn't want me to talk to him,so I tried every possible way to convince him that he is so good. As told earlier, my family was not in favor of talking to boys and that too a lot. She told me to cut ties with him, block him from every social media platform and delete his number. I cried a lot. I told him everything and requested him not to stop talking to me. He is so nice that he told me to obey my mother. At first, I was extremely shattered and questioned him if he could live by not talking to me. After that what he said touched my heart, and my respect for him grew more. He said that whether we talk or not we are always connected by soul. I will never ever get such a pure hearted soul anywhere. That's why I was scared of losing him. I couldn't afford to lose him at any cost. I developed insecurity, so I told him not to make any other best friends. He asked me why there can't be multiple besties. I tried to explain to him that I don't believe in sharing besties and I had a fear that he'll leave me. He took a vow that he'll never leave me when someone else comes. But still I couldn't let him make someone else as his best friend. Now you all might say I'm selfish, but if you want to call me selfish then let it be. I just care about him and nothing else. I used to obey my mother every time but this time I disobeyed my mother. I lied to her that I have cut ties with him but I talked to him at college and started talking to him in messages through another account of instagram which was safe from my mother. One day, my younger brother saw my messages that I sent to him, he told me that he'll discuss this with my mother. I requested him and tried to convince him. Atlast, with great difficulty he agreed.

Melancholic Journey

My journey was going well until one day he stopped seeing my messages and didn't answer my calls. Maybe because previously, I told him in a joking way that I'm irritated by boys. I myself don't know the exact reason and he is not even telling me that left me heartbroken. I was shocked and shattered into pieces. I couldn't control my emotions. Seeing him happily posting stories made me devastated. In the night, I cried and in the morning I lied to myself that some day, he'll message me but it did not happen. Each day passed with a hope that he'll talk to me. I started having anxiety attacks and frustration. I couldn't concentrate on anything and started searching for ways to move on. Listening to many counseling videos, I still couldn't overcome this and that's when I felt a need to write my story to share with you all my pain. A spring of emotions travel through my mind. Like a time traveller, I've become an emotional traveller riding through the emotions of everyday life. Have you heard of melody turning into cacophony ? A Daffodil changing into a thorny plant due to sheer suffering caused by human beings. Many a times, life takes a turn which lead to an unexpected maze. A maze full of unknown ways to make you confused at each step and scared to not to take a wrong path makes all the more stressful. It's a fact that humans harm humans who are inhuman by their actions. It's true that a reaction is a cause of an action but emotions are just like an overflowing bucket of water that continues to flow. Irrespective of the visitors who carry a lot of opinions about people, without their will to make useless gossip to pass their time. These emotions talk a lot while being silent, sometimes not letting you sleep, forcing you to overthink, making you despair and as lonely as a cloud. Making your breath as heavy as the volumes of the books. A storm of the mind is actually stronger than the sea with waves of the mind blocking your soul to peace, struggling to survive where Darwin's theory is of no use is the psychological pumping in the mind. No matter how hard you try to solve the tangled threads. For a moment, You may solve the tangled threads But, tangled threads in the mind cannot be solved easily. Going through the pinching pain swirling in the mind witnessing the strangling fights in the mind and heart, uneasiness of the forming of thoughts and waiting for the shedding of fogg, to clear the vision ahead. Bubbles of emotions glide like a rollercoaster, sometimes fast, sometimes slow which are unpredictable as the weather. A pain that consist of every spectrum of colour that a poet can only understand. Poets are badly judged by people. Poets are not the one to be judged because they are one to bleed their words to make the readers feel their pain and let them know that they are not alone. In the journey of pain and suffering, measuring the Platonic and Socrates art to the contemporary world is not an easy task. I'm struggling between pen and thoughts to decorate on the blank life which is not able to reflect from outside.

Affliction And The End

My story reflects unexplained pain and suffering being left out by my best friend. That's how Besties became strangers now. I still wonder what happened to his vow when he promised to not to leave me ? If he ever reads my writings, I want him to answer this question of mine. But It is said that every story does not have a happy ending because it's not a melo- dramatic film. I end my story here by expressing my heartfelt gratitude to my readers for patiently reading my story

9 798887 175539

Printed by Libri Plureos GmbH in Hamburg, Germany